Under The Sun

Kay Ford

BookLeaf Publishing

Presentation by *BookLeaf Publishing*

Web: www.bookleafpub.com

E-mail: info@bookleafpub.com

ISBN: 9789357448468

First edition 2022

What Does The Sky Mean?

Underneath this expanse of invisible, important
things
where dust flies at the speed of exotic math
we open our mouths wide so you can fill them
with shaking throbs
of tambourines.
And back and forth we run
squeezing the necks of each other,
pounding chests,
witnesses of bruised backs.
With squinted eyes, we lift the hems of our skirts
to dance and expose
deep, purple bowels.
We reach for sharp things when you spread your
banner over us.
Your language blurs our dimension.
Fold us into your compass.
Unravel our orbit.

That

That you had to slowly sojourn each grocery
store aisle
to look at the pictures on food and non food
items because
you could not read.

That, you told stories with words of glowing
pinks of Texas summer sunsets.

That I remember your low hum, how it crowded
itself against
the kitchen window screen and wept its way into
my lungs
after making an exchange in the walls of my
throat.

That the hymns of your days caused you to
know the formation of letters in
peculiar ways.

Not Four but Nine

It was a wet September,
on a day when red and brown leaves stuck to the
curb.
The paleness of the sky seemed to weak for the
world,
and I knew I would never see you again.

The ninth one is the cruelest.

Untitled

They were all caked in mud, those letters you
sent. After I unwrapped
the crumbling, washed out golden fabric you
bundled them in,
I tried to piece your ideas together:

I never found that garden. The address you sent
was not registered.
But then again I did have to collage the pieces of
the map
that I got from the man with the twisted mouth.
His drool loomed thick as he spoke of an orange
longitude.

And your jewelry was never accounted for:
I visited the shopkeeper, and though his fingers
shined in the dark,
he yelled promises of never receiving your
package of gems and gold.

And to think of all those screams I gave you.

No Wonder I Cannot Breathe

I cheat on you all the time.

Because it scrapes against my bosom and beats
and
yanks me down and
flies far out to forbidden places highly decorated
with neon colors and
brassy, busty trumpets and
sleek laughter that fills my mouth and
drowning thunder that calls my name and
moist cake that singes my skin where
I end up filling cup after cup after cup to
wander in the womb of a concrete sky.

Untitled

He scribbled out little lies
and parted his lips to form cold, gray falsehoods.
I tried to paint them in my diary using complex
color schemes
so I could warn the others.
I made sure to hang balloons with no helium
along the path.

Only flying things have wings.

I tried to rearrange his words and make new
definitions.
Sometimes the want of a thing is desperate, long
and aching.

I stacked a pile of scribbled lies that I set out
with Thursday's trash. I have forgotten the sound
of the words that pass through your lips.

Untitled

His hips were wide.

They blocked my view of the part of the carnival
that had the Ferris wheel lit up
that freed screams of pleasure.

And so we began our conversation of lights:
He rippled his waves and I flicked my particles;
tiny matter stretched out to roar its legends
inside me,
running amuck
down my forearm
to my palms
to make noon day
and capture darkness
in the roundness of my ankles.
I cannot tell you where.

untitled

My memory is thick with phantoms that
fill my head
who scratch out their stories inside the bleeding
walls of
my mind with quick hands
that become blurred fierce fingers
that construct expert sentences
that are long, compound, weighty
and reach the sky of my brain
and just when I think I have one cornered
it disappears and
I am left chasing something of the wind.

If I had to choose you or the sunshine,
I would learn to live in darkness.

untitled

I need the strength from your hello

to turn my tongue a courageous lime, green
to soak my heart in crowns of emeralds that have
been worn by kings
who have conquered the volcano people
to still me and let your song pass through me
to cover me in your oil full of hallelujah

untitled

People come out of the organized structure of
your sounds.
You have tasted the lining of me.
Men with clashing swords spill from your
phonemes.
All of my blood and its meat knows you.
It just takes eyes that beg
to split legs.
In all the light you multiply yourself,
my hundred, handed lover.

untitled

We arose from our nakedness only for ashes to
swirl around us
and your pretty lips sang drunkenness while I
bent down to
wonder why there were bells around my ankles.
Had I known that you would spread me so wide
to fit civilizations
made of rejected stone inside me, filling my
belly with pale horses,
that slowed me down and made me tired and
thirsty,
that neighed and whinnied all night and never
rested,
whose parade of hooves trampled and whispered
and
shifted, I would have never entered your tightly
coiled cave to eat your dust.
Now I know this is the last end of the sky.

Aquino Properties

333 - 8515

Rethinking all the memories turn you a tangerine color.

I am awed that forever can be broken by your tongue.

All those things you said are stuck behind traffic lights, blinking...blinking.

I want to eat all the places you have been, swallow everything you have touched. Bury me with all the days that have held you and confined you to space. Let twilight snatch you and bring you to me.

blinking, blinking, blinking...

Under The Sun

I remember you as a time of day,
a house of yes,
in ten thousand tiny pieces,
in the anatomy of purple,
as daylight's unblemished construction,
as a gasping burgundy,
while digesting the rhythm of your things,
amidst the tangling of frail fairytales,
while learning linear assemblies,
when counting your numbers,
as I became something else under the sun.

untitled

"Girl, the old lady sent the notes to flying sparrows and
we 'bout had a fit.
She pulled a coin purse out of the bigger bag, the one with pink sequins,
and told us that the feast would be extravagant.
Most of us couldn't sit idly by only to stare at the sky so the crowd dwindled. I kept wondering, like dang, like man, she didn't have to let it all blow in the wind like that. But something inside me said the wind would know how high those birds flew. So I went around making sure everyone had water and that people kept their ticket that had been stamped. And, ooo, girl it felt like forever, but down the way we heard muffled noises getting louder and that flock of sparrows gathering above our heads.
But then violence broke out. People who had left wanted to come back and claim their stamped ticket. Sheesh, those tickets were gone. I mean it was pure madness. I held on to my stamped ticket and thanked the good Lord for sparrows, girl. I mean, it was something. Any who, I thought I'd call you cause I have been looking for you. I don't see you. I remember you had

your stamped ticket, and that was all you needed.

Make me wait.

Hotline Service

None of these buttons work.

And now everyone hides their hands. But I saw savage spit being propelled through the air as it encased comfortable rage.

Bizarre

You ask me about the dissection of a prayer, and I reply by describing the separation of dense dungeons. I taught you how to untie them, before you let the light inside. You do not have to chop off their ends; spread them out. They may start out parallel to each other, but give them space. It works best if they are exposed. Their beginning height and weight are of little importance. They can start out hollow, facing various directions, or hang. They will all eventually rise.

Their entrance is not always smooth, though when done in truth, the surrounding entering cavity becomes covered with a thin layer of hardened resin. Do not neglect the small passage ways.

Pay attention to the lower and middle levels. Study the architecture before entering. Understand the dimness, in that order. Analyze the petition before the colony collapses.

Lay it all out in the temple. Stand back. Set it all on fire.

The Keeper's Wife

At thirty I married you.
I cried all the time and built a harp to settle
inside my sound.
Steadying my head, I studied the exponents of
your curriculum.
Whispered , a thousand times a thousand, I
never blinked.

At 42 I glistened with your rescue.
I wanted your boundary to be my jurisdiction.
Always and always and always.
How can I have your moments?

At 44 you brightened your jubilee,
You showed me coasts and rivers,
And you have been a golden enduring.
The trees high overhead laud you.

You do not tarry.
The gates are raised; the smoke yet rises; our
bowls are yet full.
You have pulled me down deep,
into a new mud.
The grasshoppers are waning and the store house
has plenty for the coming season

of festivals;
I have grown an older champion in your
besetting.
When you come down through the narrow
way
Please call out to me,
And I will come with heaving bosom to meet
you
As far as east is from west
As far as north is from south.

untitled

I love your phone call

to interrupt my day and build me a castle of
details that I inspect to understand how they
form flat foundations in my mind, so I can swing
from their tall balconies later when butterflies
explode inside me so

call me

all the time so I can hear the cadence of your
voice to memorize it and mimic it in the night so
I can fall asleep to its lullaby.

www.ingramcontent.com/pod-product-compliance
Lightning Source LLC
Chambersburg PA
CBHW051723130826
49812CB00034B/1319

* 9 7 8 9 3 5 7 4 4 8 4 6 8 *

Thoughts From The Stour Banks

Glenn Collins

BookLeaf Publishing

Presentation by *BookLeaf Publishing*

Web: www.bookleafpub.com

E-mail: info@bookleafpub.com

ISBN: 9789357213158

First edition 2023

Workplace Friends

Workplace friends are a saving grace,
A grain of calm in a mutinous place.
Colleagues they forever come and go,
But when a friendship bonds you just know.
And when the time comes to bid goodbye,
You wish them well and do not cry.
Something I pondered with this last line,
Where would I be without these friends of mine.

Time

The Time has come for lowered guards,
Check the stakes and play the cards.
Scared or brave, make the call,
Play it safe? Or, go for all?
Time doesn't wait, I've come to see.
After all the past took from me.
So a question asked, for the answer I'll wait...
Is it time that holds our fate?

How've You Been?

Come walk with me,
Through a workplace scene.
19 months...
Tell me, How've you been?

Masks and sanitiser
A reminder of what we went through
Distanced desks,
Old office but this is new.

Glance left and right
Catch a smile, share some memes.
We're back to our normal,
Sharing the love between friends and teams

# #

Hashtags, follow backs,
Watching movies on a mobile phone.
Over 2000 followers but,
You've never felt more alone.

Complain about a life,
But advertise it on the 'gram
In love, fuming, ooh drama!
OMG - DM me fam?!

So it seems to me,
We traded reality,
For connectivity
Trading social for socials
Preferring to Snapchat
Than meet to chat.
"A quick game on the PC?"
Rather than debate PC over coffee

The Beautiful Game

"It's our year" is the dream,
Of every fan, of every team.
It is The Beautiful Game,
Football is it's name.

A pie and A pint,
The pre-match ritual.
The singing of the crowd,
The togetherness is spiritual.

When it comes down to the nitty gritty,
It doesn't matter if your Arsenal or Spurs
or even Man. City.
Because we all feel the same,
The moment our striker takes aim,
We're fans, United, by the beautiful game

Perfect Contrast

The Clutch drops,
Engine Pops,
The Adrenaline rush is surreal.

It's perfectly contrast
A bike moving so fast
But time seems to remain still

Lockdown Thoughts

Objectivising depression as motivation,
Beautifying friendships for appreciation.
Revisiting loneliness and desperation,
Incomprehensibility of adaptation.
However, a revolution in confidence,
Accelerated the differences,
Of harmonious, self satisfaction.

The Forbidden Tree

On the outskirts of the town,
Along the lane you mustn't go down.
Stands the old Forbidden Tree,
Dark and enchanting as can be.

A presence, menacing and foreboding,
It whistles and rustles in the wind.
It inches ever closer, now almost goading,
As if to lure you in.

"I am The Forbidden Tree,
And in these fields I stand,
A warning to all Enmity,
As a defender, of this land."

Last Summer

We didn't know it was your last summer,
Until the joy turned to despair.
Then the smiles turned to tears,
Gazing upon your empty chair.
Physically you're not here,
But I know your always there,
Your laughter fills the hallway,
Your scent lingers in the air

Storm

Batten down the hatches,
Lock up all the doors,
There's a storm front coming,
Like no other before.

As the waves come crashing,
And the rain starts lashing,
The torrent is gathering power,
So, sit tight, and wait each passing hour.

Because when the storm has passed,
And the calm is here at last,
Remember this lifelong truth...
You must endure the rough,
To appreciate the smooth

Want Away

My mind is burning, with these thoughts inside,
All I'm learning is there's nowhere to hide.
Can I roll away like an ocean tide?
Start again on the other side.

All You Do

Whilst there may be doubts in everyone,
Keep on going until you've done.
If you keep the strength to pull through
It will shine in all you do

13 - Unlucky for some

So, how can it be,
That 13 is unlucky?
It's just a number,
Written with a 1 and 3.

But a look through history,
Tells tales of tragedy,
Memories of misery,
all connected to 13.

And if the 13th should be Friday,
Take extra care or even hide away.
Because a menace awaits, upon that date,
And it may just seal your fate.

The Gardens of Home

Recalling memories of my childhood,
The endless fields and Poulders Park.
The friendships of the neighbourhood,
Kicking footballs after dark,

These are more than happy memories,
It's a heart forged in Kentish stone.
Whenever I smell Lavender and Berries,
It reminds me of my home.

Writer's Block

Tap the pen on the table,
Scroll through apps on the phone.
Search for something inspirational,
To find the words you can hone.

Pick a word at random,
Think up a clever rhyme,
Whatever rhymes with tandem?
Oh well better luck next time.

Come back three days later,
And you're up against the clock.
The desperation's now greater,
But you still have writer's block

City Lights

Against the back drop of sunset,
The shimmering streetlight,
Create such beautiful contrast,
A picture perfect, artist's delight.

The reflections in the river,
A beauty that makes me quiver.
The wonders, of this fair city,
Illuminated and oh so pretty.

More Tea?

It's more than just a drink,
It's an opportunity to think.
A catch up with old friends,
Or build bridges and make amends

The first brew of the day,
Hit's the spot and sits just right,
Whether it's PG Tips or an Earl Grey.
Get's you ready for a daily plight.

When I wake up, Or just before sleep,
Coco or Coffee you can keep.
No matter where I'll be,
I'll answer affirmatively when asked...

More Tea?

Everything's Changing

With a click of a button,
We can find out anything that's known,
Do the shopping, pay our bills,
Without leaving home.

Everything's changing,
From what we use to know,
Those days are not returning,
We've only got one way to go.

Anxiety

The cold sweats in the middle of night,
Shaking and trembling nothing feels right.
Trying to breathe as my chest gets tight,
Every sense saying I'm doomed to my plight.

I can get through this, I'm sure.
I've done it a hundred times before.
Feel my heart pounding through my chest,
This anxiety won't kill me, but it's doing it's best.

When it ends and possible causes are mused,
There's no trace on the body,
It's not battered or bruised.
It's all in the mind, be it overused,
Or just misused and abused.

Christmas in Sandwich

Crisp winters days and frosty nights.
Smell of chimneys and those festive lights,
The countdown has begun.
Hug loved ones and see old friends,
Drinks with colleagues, fun never ends.

Times have changed over the years,
For missing loved one's we shed tears.
Toast their names with a glass of wine,
And that delicious feast, on which we dine.
All these things I will always remember,
In the joy of a Cold December.

For You

Friendship is the fuse that lights the spark,
That can give you strength to pull through.
There were times when the road was dark,
But you always knew just what to do,
I never would've come this far,
If it wasn't for you.

My Friends are the best of me,
I know that with certainty,
A crystalline clarity,
Though I don't always show my gratitude.
But please know, this much is true,
I won't use a tired old platitude,
But what I should do,
Is use my last few lines,
As a dedication, just for you.

www.ingramcontent.com/pod-product-compliance
Lightning Source LLC
Chambersburg PA
CBHW051723130826
49812CB00034B/1318
* 9 7 8 9 3 5 7 2 1 3 1 5 8 *